# James Harden

## The Inspirational Story of Basketball Superstar James Harden

**Copyright 2015 by Bill Redban - All rights reserved.**

This document is geared towards providing exact and reliable information in regards to the topic and issue covered. The publication is sold with the idea that the publisher is not required to render accounting, officially permitted, or otherwise, qualified services. If advice is necessary, legal or professional, a practiced individual in the profession should be ordered.

In no way is it legal to reproduce, duplicate, or transmit any part of this document in either electronic means or in printed format. Recording of this publication is strictly prohibited and any storage of this document is not allowed unless with written permission from the publisher. All rights reserved.

The information provided herein is stated to be truthful and consistent, in that any liability, in terms of inattention or otherwise, by any usage or abuse of any policies, processes, or directions contained within is the solitary and utter responsibility of the recipient reader. Under no circumstances will any legal responsibility or blame be held against the publisher for any reparation, damages, or monetary loss due to the information herein, either directly or indirectly.

The information herein is offered for informational purposes solely, and is universal as so. The presentation of the information is without contract or any type of guarantee assurance.

The trademarks that are used are without any consent, and the publication of the trademark is without permission or backing by the trademark owner. All trademarks and brands within this book are for clarifying purposes only and are the owned by the owners themselves, not affiliated with this document.

# Table Of Contents

Introduction

Chapter 1: Youth & Family Life

Chapter 2: College

Chapter 3: Professional Life

Chapter 4: Personal Adult Life

Chapter 5: Philanthropic/Charitable Acts

Chapter 6: Legacy, Potential & Inspiration

Conclusion

# Introduction

As the title already implies, this is a short book about [The Inspirational Story of Basketball Superstar James Harden] and how he rose from his life in Compton, Los Angeles to becoming one of today's leading and most-respected basketball players. In his rise to superstardom, James has inspired not only the youth, but fans of all ages throughout the world.

This book also portrays the struggles that James has had to overcome during his early childhood years, his teen years, and up until he became what he is today. A notable source of inspiration is James' service to the community and his strong connection with the fans of the sport. He continues to serve as a humble, fun-loving superstar in a sport that glorifies flashy plays and mega personalities.

Combining a deadly step-back, incredible footwork, a feathery jump-shot, and high basketball IQ, James has shown the ability to completely take over a game. From being a young phenom to becoming one of the greatest guards of his generation, you'll learn here how this man has risen to the ranks of the best basketball players today.

Thanks again for grabbing this book. Hopefully you can take some of the examples from James' story and apply them to your own life!

## Chapter 1:

## Youth & Family Life

The world welcomed James Edwards Harden, Jr. on August 26th, 1989. He was born in Los Angeles, California to father James Harden Sr. and mother Monja Willis. At the time of young James' birth, his father was enrolled in the United States Navy but later found his way down a path of drugs and multiple stints in jail. Because of this, James grew to rely on his mother and didn't have much association with his absentee father, later dropping the Jr. from his name.

James' mother, Monja, was a rock solid foundation for her son and she held a job as an administrator for the AT&T office located in Pasadena, California. James was the third child of his family but was more than ten years younger than his two siblings. His half-brother, Akili Roberson, was a very impressive quarterback for local Locke High School. He went on to play for the University of Kansas and was inspirational to young James.

James grew up in the Compton area of Los Angeles, specifically in the Rancho Dominguez locality - an area that has produced many talented athletes over the years. James was like his older brother Akili, in that he possessed natural athleticism to go along with above-average height. He was drawn to basketball, as many youngsters in the Southern California area are, and was lucky to have very good competition around him as he was growing up.

An obstacle that James had to overcome during his youth was that he suffered from the medical condition of asthma. He learned to accommodate his medical needs with an inhaler and did not let it affect how hard he played out on the court. Aside from being a solid student, James also enjoyed playing video games and watching basketball on television. He was a fan of UCLA basketball specifically, a college basketball powerhouse that was not far from his home.

Rancho Dominguez was not as dangerous as some other parts of Compton, but it was certainly not a safe area. There was a still a high number of property thefts and car/house break-ins when James was growing up. Because of this, Monja decided to send James outside the neighborhood for his education. James would enroll in Artesia High School in Lakewood, a suburb about fifteen minutes away from Rancho Dominguez. Monja looked out for her children and it ended up paying dividends for James and the family's future.

Not only was Artesia a well-respected school in the area, but it also featured one of the best basketball programs in Southern California. The school had developed a reputation for producing talented players such as Tom Tolbert and Jason Kapono, among others. The varsity coach, Scott Pera, was a top-tier high school coach who possessed a talent in developing raw players.

James would make the starting line-up of the varsity team as a sophomore and was able to average double digits in scoring. Artesia won almost thirty games during the season and showed great potential for the future. Between his sophomore and junior year, James hit a growth spurt and he noticeably improved his jump shot in the off-season. By the time his junior season started, Coach Pera was looking for James to have a more pronounced role in the team's offense.

A naturally unselfish player, James did not want to step on any toes and had to be encouraged to play aggressively at times. However, the players on the team believed in James' abilities and most importantly, Coach Pera saw and harnessed James' playmaking talents so that they could mutually benefit.

James responded by leading the Pioneers to the State Championship and a 33-1 record. He personally averaged almost 20 points per game and his ability to take over in the clutch was beginning to develop. He would use this momentum and confidence boost to further develop his game in the AAU circuit, becoming an all-around player who could score upwards of twenty points in a game, as well as lock down an opposing player for stretches at a time.

Towards the end of the summer, James had a statement game in Las Vegas, when he scored almost 70 points in back-to-back games. Not only did he accomplish such a difficult feat, but the opposing teams had big name studs such as Kevin Love, Michael Beasley, Austin Freeman, and Nolan Smith.

Coming into his senior season with high expectations and his confidence at an all-time high, James was able to lead his team to another state championship, this time under coach Loren Grover. They won 33 games once again and James showed true comfort as the star player for the team. Arguably just as important, James was able to help nurture burgeoning stars Renardo Sidney and Malik Story, who were both younger than James. His leadership put Artesia in a position to stay at the top even after he would leave.

During his youth, James looked up to San Antonio Spurs star guard, Manu Ginobili. As both were left-handed nifty players, James tried to implement many of Manu's moves into his own repertoire. As he began to develop into his own, scouts and coaches noted that James' basketball IQ was very impressive for his age.

## Chapter 2:

## College

Because James had such a decorated high school and AAU career, he had some leverage with his multitude of scholarship offers. With Monja moving to Phoenix because her mother had just passed away and left her a home in her will, along with his former coach and mentor, Scott Pera, now working as an assistant, Arizona State University was the clear-cut favorite in James' mind.

Even with James' arrival, the Arizona State Sun Devils were not seriously considered to be more than a .500 team in the competitive Pac-10. James would be counted on to lead the team to new heights and he was ready to embrace that role. He would go on to lead the team to an overall record of 21-13, along with point guard Derek Glasser and forward Ty Pendergraph. Statistically, James led the team with almost an eighteen points per game average to go along with more than two steals per game. His three-point percentage was over 40% making him a deadly shooter by college basketball standards.

Surprising to most around the country, the Sun Devils were in consideration for the NCAA Tournament by the end of the regular season. Despite the fact that they slightly missed one of the last tournament spots, Arizona State was still able to make some noise in the NIT Tournament and well exceeded the outside expectations put on them. For James, he finished his freshman campaign being named to the First-Team All Pac-10 team and was a no-brainer for the conference All-Freshman Team.

By the beginning of his sophomore season, James had grown into a celebrity on campus, as many of the students would wear memorabilia sporting phrases about James - including shirts that read, "Die Harden Fan". Tempe was embracing James and he would use the momentum to his advantage. In a game against UTEP, James dropped forty points and completely took over the game. This performance also placed James into consideration as one of the best scorers in the entire conference. He finished the season with an average of over twenty points per game and led the Pac-10 in total steals for the second consecutive season.

As a sign of recognition, James was voted as the Pac-10 Player of the Year and was given national attention by the media and even the underground college basketball fans. He was even named a consensus All-American. For the season, ASU won twenty games and were able to make it into the NCAA Tournament as a sixth seed, but lost in the second round to third seeded powerhouse, Syracuse.

After the college basketball season ended, it became apparent that James had potential to play in the NBA and he seized the opportunity. He would declare for the NBA Draft after only his sophomore season. To help him in his guidance and negotiations, James decided to go with accomplished agent Rob Pelinka.

# Chapter 3:

## Professional Life

### First Season

As there was little doubt that Oklahoma's Blake Griffin would be selected with the number one overall pick by the Los Angeles Clippers, James was hoping that he would follow soon after. The Oklahoma City Thunder were very impressed by James' maturity and skill set, and General Manager Sam Presti decided that James was their guy. With the number three pick in the draft, James was chosen by the Thunder as the first player to be drafted by the franchise since its move from Seattle.

The franchise was still in rebuilding mode after drafting talented players like Russell Westbrook, Kevin Durant and Jeff Green and hoped that James could become another piece in the rebuilding process. The team had only won 23 games in the previous season and there was not much outside expectations for the team to make the playoffs in the loaded Western Conference.

James was given more than twenty minutes per game as a rookie, showing that he could be an integral part of the Thunder's rotation. In this limited amount of playing time, James was still able to average around ten points per game and was named to the NBA All-Rookie Second Team. His role as the sixth man of the team allowed James to provide instant-offense off the bench for a team that desperately needed scoring while its starters were resting.

The team finished the regular season with a surprising fifty win total and was able to make the Western Conference Playoffs. They faced the Los Angeles Lakers in the first round and came up short, but they were competitive in almost every game in the series. James was able to really show promise as a scorer and defender during the highly anticipated series. He scored eighteen points in Game 3 and had a couple of steals in Game 4.

## Second Season

James entered his second season with a feeling of belonging and the team designated him as one of the key pieces moving forward. He played in every regular season game and averaged more than twelve points per game. He would play even better in the Playoffs than he did in the regular season, as he raised his scoring average to thirteen points per game and shot almost 50% from the field.

James was also starting to develop a reputation as more than just a scorer, he was a play-maker. A play-maker is a rarity on the NBA level. The big difference between a scorer and a play-maker is that a play-maker can get his own shot but also has the awareness and ability to make the other players on the court better by creating opportunities for them.

James' three point shooting really opened up the floor and spread defenses thin when they played against the three-headed monster of a Durant-Westbrook-Harden line-up. The team would win 55 games for the season and grab first place of the Northwest Division, surpassing outside expectations once again - a trend you probably have noticed now for teams that James plays on. In the playoffs, the Thunder would make it all the way to the Western Conference Finals, beating the Denver Nuggets and Memphis Grizzlies along the way.

After meeting the red-hot Dallas Mavericks in the Conference Finals, Dirk Nowitzki and company were a little too much for the inexperienced Thunder, as they took ahold of the pace and controlled the tempo of the series, even though all five games were close.

## Third Season

Despite their young core, the Thunder entered the 2011-12 season as one of the favorites to contend for a championship. Their star players were still well below their prime and the fan base felt optimistic in Oklahoma City.

The team would go on to win the Northwest Division once again and James took his role as the Sixth Man to another level. He had multiple offensive explosions during the season, including a 40 point game against the Phoenix Suns. He was able to score over twenty points in fourteen different games and had three games of more than thirty points.

Furthermore, he was getting these points in a very efficient manner. Not only was he only playing a little over thirty minutes a game, but James was also second in the entire NBA in true shooting percentage and effective field goal percentage.

This display of dominance led James to being named the NBA's Sixth Man of the Year and put him among the top fifteen or so scorers in the entire league. James was also the second youngest player to ever win the award, showing that he could probably take on a bigger role for the team. As most players who win the award are in their prime or on the back end of their career, rarely does a man in his first few seasons win it.

Because of a setback from an elbow to the head by Metta World Peace, James was forced to miss a number of games because of a concussion. However, he returned for the Playoffs and picked up right where he left off. The Thunder entered the first round in a rematch against the Dallas Mavericks, this time sweeping Dallas handily. James showed that he had superstar potential when he came through in the biggest game of the series, scoring 29 points in Game 4.

From there, the Thunder beat the Los Angeles Lakers and James showed defensive brilliance as he was assigned to guard Kobe Bryant in clutch moments of the series. He had eight steals in only five games. After Oklahoma City beat the Lakers in five games, they met the well-respected San Antonio Spurs in the Western Conference Finals.

The Thunder were able to harness their youth and naivete into a four game winning streak after being dominated in the first two games of the series. James would score twenty points in the Game 5 victory and hit multiple clutch baskets. This series victory would earn the Thunder a berth into the NBA Finals to play against the Miami Heat.

The favorite, Miami Heat, would beat the Thunder in relatively easy fashion but the Thunder had taken another big step forward as a franchise, finally winning their conference. The future looked bright in Oklahoma City and the fan base couldn't have been any more proud of the effort put forth by the squad.

As a surprise to many around the league, James was asked to join teammates Russell Westbrook and Kevin Durant on the 2012 Olympic Team as one of the last players added to the roster. This served notice that James was considered to be one of the elite players in the game and that he was on the same level as the guys he went to London with. The team would go on to be undefeated in the Olympics and brought a Gold Medal back home to the United States.

# Fourth Season

Just before the 2012-13 season kicked off, the Thunder were looking to make a deal with James for a contract extension and a secured role as the sixth man for the team. However, James believed that he could provide a bigger role and the Thunder worked out a trade with the Houston Rockets. This show of faith and confidence would lead James into a position that he would be grateful for. This foresight was questioned by many around the league, but James did not disappoint.

Daryl Morey, the Rockets general manager, showed confidence in James by calling him a "foundational player" for the team's future. After signing a max-level contract with the Rockets soon after arriving, James turned into a straight up stud. His abilities were on display instantly, as his first game posted statistics including 37 points, 12 assists, 6 rebounds, and 4 steals.

His first performance as a Rocket put him into legendary company as the only player in franchise history to tie Hakeem Olajuwon's stat-line of 37/12. He would go on to score 45 points in his second game for a combined 82 in his first two games - a historic start for any player still adjusting to a new team. His play during the first week of the season would garner him the Western Conference Player of the Week award.

James would continue this momentum and post games of 40-plus points as well as a few double-digit assist games. Most importantly, he provided the organization with a go-to player who could take over a game and lead the young core around him. James would go on to win another Player of the Week award and even had a streak of scoring 25 points in fourteen straight games - a franchise record.

This rise to superstardom, gave James a position on the Western Conference All-Star Team and he even scored fifteen points in the game. After the All-Star Break, James would go on to set a career-high of 46 points against his former team, the Oklahoma City Thunder.

The season served as a coming-out party for James and showed many doubters around the league that he made the right decision to ask for a bigger role in his occupation. He was a superstar talent that deserved a superstar role, and the Rockets sure were glad about that. His season average of almost 26 points per game and almost 2 steals per game were both career highs.

The team would eventually make the playoffs as the eighth seed but did not make it past the first round matchup against the Oklahoma City Thunder. However, James and the Rockets were able to win two games in the series and he performed admirably despite having flu-like symptoms in the last two games of the series. His postseason averages of more than 26 points, almost 7 rebounds, 5 assists, and two steals, were playoff career highs for him.

His 2012-13 campaign earned him All-NBA Third Team honors and placed him in the conversation among the best shooting guards in the NBA.

## Fifth Season

After signing center Dwight Howard in free agency, Rockets management felt like they could begin pushing to create one of the best rosters in the league. Dwight and James became one of the best duos in the game and the best guard-center offensive combination.

The team greatly improved from the previous season, winning 54 games and earning the fifth seed in the Western Conference Playoffs. The team would eventually lose to the Portland Trail Blazers in a closely fought series, but the future was bright in Houston and the Rockets could only improve as their duo became more comfortable with each other.

James was recognized as one of the best players in the game when he was named to the 2014 All-NBA First Team, a very sought after accomplishment by players around the league.

# Chapter 4:

# Personal Adult Life

James has developed a well-rounded character and has a like-able personality both on and off the court. He serves as one of the more intriguing stars in the league because of his fashion sense, iconic beard, and marketable personality. James has appeared in a number of commercials, including ones for Foot Locker and BBVA. His sense of humor shines through when he gives interviews and his stoic expressions always make for a great laugh.

James has publicly stated that he is a Christian. He has talked about his faith, saying things like he wants to "thank God for everything he has done" in his life. Throughout all of the struggles that James has had to overcome during his childhood and youth, he has been able to put his family into a position of success and abundance. This could have only been accomplished through staying humble and a confidence that could not be broken.

As for James' iconic beard, he started growing it during his college days because he was too lazy to shave. He maintained a relatively shorter beard during college and even in the beginning of his professional career, but later went all-out with the full, sculpted look to go along with the mo-hawk. This appearance is one of the most memorable amongst casual fans and James has developed his own "look", something that a lot of men wish they could achieve.

Throughout his rise to stardom, fans have become creative, making t-shirts, fake beards, and posters to show their support for James. Seeing phrases like "Fear the Beard" are common at any Houston Rockets home game.

# Chapter 5:

## Philanthropic/Charitable Acts

Throughout James' stops in his short time as a professional, he has made sure to give back to the communities that support him - whether it be Oklahoma City, Houston, or his hometown of Los Angeles.

Recently, alongside teammate Jeremy Lin, James participated in a shopping spree for select children from disadvantaged families. The spree was funded by James and was done in the name of the holiday spirit. James participated in this with his mother, Monja, and it made a huge impact in the lives of the selected families. Not only was the financial help appreciated, but the action was very generous and it gave hope to the children who were affected by it.

## Chapter 6:

## Legacy, Potential & Inspiration

James' career is still young but we can learn much from his journey. Not only is he a prime example of succeeding despite being from a single parent household, he also shows us that believing in yourself can go a long way.

Whether it was giving himself permission to be a little more selfish at Artesia High, deciding to trust in himself in a superstar role, or even growing a beard that other people might view as "weird", James' confidence shines through. His belief in his own abilities allows other teammates to trust him with the ball, knowing that he will eventually make the right decision most of the time. Because of this, they find themselves with open shots and easy looks based on his penetration and court vision.

The future in Houston remains to be seen, but what is certain is that James is one of those generational players who is bigger than basketball. His persona brings fans into the stadium and buying his jersey. He is the type of star player that general managers dream of and a son that his mother, Monja, has become extremely proud of.

With the aging Dwyane Wade and Kobe Bryant, the NBA is looking to hand James the torch as the premier shooting guard in the league. While James is still quite young and there are still other promising shooting guards such as Demar DeRozan and Klay Thompson, James has shown that his work ethic and basketball IQ will always keep him relevant and at the top - much like one of his childhood role models, Manu Ginobili.

# Conclusion

I hope this book was able to help you gain inspiration from the life of James Harden, one of the best players currently playing in the National Basketball Association.

The rise and fall of a star is often the cause for much wonder. But most stars have an expiration date. In basketball, once a star player reaches his mid- to late-thirties, it is often time to contemplate retirement. What will be left in people's minds about that fading star? In James' case, people will remember how he led a franchise in their journey towards a championship. He will be remembered as the guy who plucked his franchise from obscurity, helped them build their image, and honed his own image along the way.

James has also inspired so many people because he is the star who never fails to connect with fans and give back to the less fortunate. Noted for his ability to impose his will on any game, he

is a joy to watch on the basketball court. Last but not least, he's remarkable for remaining simple and firm with his principles in spite of his immense popularity.

Hopefully you learned some great things about James in this book and are able to apply some of the lessons that you've learned to your own life! Good luck in your own journey!

Printed in Great Britain
by Amazon

# Sunny Beach Travel Guide

*Sightseeing, Hotel, Restaurant & Shopping Highlights*

James Simon

Copyright © 2018, Astute Press
All Rights Reserved.

No part of this publication may be reproduced, stored in a retrieval system, or transmitted, in any form or by any means without the prior written permission of the publisher, nor be otherwise circulated in any form of binding or cover other than that in which it is published and without similar condition being imposed on the subsequent purchaser.

If there are any errors or omissions in copyright acknowledgements the publisher will be pleased to insert the appropriate acknowledgement in any subsequent printing of this publication.

Although we have taken all reasonable care in researching this book we make no warranty about the accuracy or completeness of its content and disclaim all liability arising from its use.

# Table of Contents

**Welcome to Sunny Beach!** ..................................................................7
- Overview ...............................................................................7
- Culture .................................................................................9
- Location & Orientation .......................................................10
- Climate & When to Visit ....................................................11

**Sightseeing Highlights** ....................................................................13
- Sunny Beach ......................................................................13
- Action Aquapark ................................................................14
- Luna Park ...........................................................................15
- Khan's Tent ........................................................................15
- Sunny Beach Night Life ....................................................16
- Nessebar ............................................................................17
- Aqua Paradise ...................................................................19
- Sveti Vlas ............................................................................19
- July Morning ......................................................................20
- Lake Pomorie .....................................................................21
- Chateau Medovo ...............................................................21
- Burgas .................................................................................22
- Sozopol ...............................................................................23
- Strandzha Nature Park .....................................................24

**Recommendations for the Budget Traveller** .....................26
- Places to Stay ....................................................................26
  - Palace Hotel .................................................................26
  - Hotel Lotus ....................................................................27
  - Aparthotel Poseidon ....................................................27
  - Ivana Palace Hotel .......................................................28
  - Hotel Avenue ................................................................28
- Places to Eat .....................................................................29
  - Morris Restaurant & Bar .............................................29
  - Lapa Lapa Restaurant .................................................30
  - Hawaii Restaurant & Bar ............................................30
  - Bolero Restaurant .......................................................31
  - Djanny ...........................................................................31
- Places to Shop ..................................................................32
  - Royal Beach Mall ........................................................32
  - Sunny Beach Promenade ...........................................33
  - Original Bulgarian Wine Shop ...................................33

Ji'votnoto & Gallery .................................................................34
Galleria Burgas........................................................................34

# Welcome to Sunny Beach!

## Overview

Sunny Beach is one of the largest resorts on the Black Sea Riviera of Bulgaria and is one of the cheapest coastal destinations in Europe. Here you can really let your hair down on a limited budget, with cocktails being sold by the bucket load at cheap prices. Sunny Beach features long, sandy, crescent-shaped beaches lined with hotels, nightspots and beach bars.

The beach carries the coveted Blue Flag rating and in the summer season, is alive with music festivals, raucous foam parties and beautiful bodies. Not surprisingly, Sunny Beach is fast gaining a reputation as one of the continent's most attractive party centres.

In the water or on land, Sunny Beach offers a plethora of fun activities. You can rent a jet ski to ride the waves or get towed on a giant banana boat or other fun inflatables, along with a few friends. Other available water sports are wakeboarding, parasailing, water-skiing and canoeing. Sunny Beach also has several water parks for cooling down, an amusement park with mini golf circuit and a casino for serious gaming.

While most visitors seek out Sunny Beach for its relentlessly outrageous party culture, the resort's nearest neighbors boast a series of completely different attractions. Explore layers of history at Nessebar, which has the world's greatest concentration of churches per square meter. The Archaeological Museum of Sozopol is home to two intriguing finds - the relic of Saint John the Baptist and the bones of the Sozopol Vampire. Sveti Vlas, which lies north of Sunny Beach, provide visitors with a quieter alternative.

Nature lovers can experience the aerial spectacle of Europe's second largest bird migration, the Via Pontica, which passes over the province of Burgas. It can be viewed from various locations near Sunny Beach, including the Poda Lagoon in the Strandzha Nature Reserve and Atonosovsko Lake, which is only 44km from Sunny Beach. Strandzha also offers outdoor activities such as hiking, cycling, horse riding and game fishing. Do not forget to visit Lake Pomorie for a rejuvenating mud bath before going home.

# Culture

Bulgaria was settled from the 6th century BC by the Thracians who were a tribe of Indo-Europeans. Rome conquered the area around 100 AD and it became part of the Eastern Roman Empire or Byzantium from 385 AD. The Slavs arrived in Bulgaria around 500 AD and in 680 AD, the country was conquered by the Bulgers, who then intermarried with the Slavs. Several centuries of tension and warfare between the Bulgarian rulers and the Byzantine Empire followed. In the 9th century, Boris I accepted the Eastern Orthodox Church, but the Byzantine Empire only recognized Bulgaria as an autonomous state late in the 12th century. From the end of the 14th century until the 19th century, Bulgaria fell under Turkish Ottoman rule, but the country gained a degree of political autonomy after the Balkan Wars. From 1946 to 1990, Bulgaria fell under communist rule, as an East Bloc country allied to the Soviet Union and during this period, Sunny Beach became a premier resort for the communist elite.

Bulgaria has a distinct folk heritage that is expressed in traditional costumes, dancing and music. Music is an important element of Bulgarian culture. Traditional instruments include the gaida (goatskin bagpipe), the kaval (flute), the gadulka (a bowed string instrument reminiscent of a violin), the tupan and the tarabuka (two different types of drums) and the tambura (a fretted lute similar to the Greek bouzouki). Bulgarians have also excelled at classical and popular music. One intriguing pagan ritual that has survived is Nestinarstvo or barefoot fire dancing, which is still practiced in various rural communities, including the village of Bulgari, in the Strandja Mountains.

The majority of the population is ethnic Bulgarian, with small percentages of Turkish and Roma. Bulgarian, the oldest written Slavic language is the native tongue of 85 percent of the population. It is also the only official language. The dominant religion is the Bulgarian Orthodox Church. About 10 percent of the population is Sunni Muslim.

## Location & Orientation

Sunny Beach is located in the eastern part of Bulgaria, along the coast of the Black Sea. It is 35km north of Burgas in the Nessebar Municipality, just north of the town of Nessebar. The setting makes it easily accessible from Turkey, Romania, Kosovo, Serbia, the Republic of Macedonia, Greece and Moldova.

The nearest airport is at Burgas and there are regular flights connecting Burgas to Sofia, the capital of Bulgaria. Additionally, you can travel from Sofia to Sunny Beach by train or bus. Sofia is connected by rail to Budapest in Hungary, Thessaloniki in Greece, Belgrade in Serbia, Bucharest in Romania and Istanbul in Turkey. A bus service also links Burgas with Turkey. By car, the shortest route from Sofia is via the A1.

By road, Sunny Beach can be reached from Istanbul in Turkey via the E80 and Route 9, a journey of 380km. From Bucharest, visitors can drive to Sunny Beach via Route 2. A regular bus service connects Sunny Beach to Nessebar, Ravda, Sveti Vlas and Elenite. There is also a ferry service connecting Sunny Beach with Nessebar, Pomorie and Sozopol.

# Climate & When to Visit

Sunny Beach enjoys a maritime climate, with the presence of the Black Sea and the mountains playing a moderating role against the harsher continental climate that occurs in much of Bulgaria. These geographical features also promote a good distribution of fresh mountain air. The World Health Organization has stated that this region has one of the world's healthiest micro-climates, which is particularly beneficial to sufferers of respiratory diseases such as asthma.

Sunny Beach experiences hot, sunny weather from June to August, with the occasional incidence of thunderstorms. During these months, day temperatures between 26 and 29 degrees Celsius are usual, with night temperatures averaging between 16 and 18 degrees Celsius. July and August are the hottest months. July is also the month when the temperature of the Black Sea is at its warmest, on average a pleasant 24 degrees Celsius. September is still fairly warm with temperatures between 24 and 15 degrees Celsius occurring on average. May is slightly cooler, with typical day temperatures around 21 degrees Celsius and night temperatures around 12 degrees Celsius.

December, January and February are the coldest months in Sunny Beach, with day averages between 6 and 8 degrees Celsius and night temperatures typically dropping to -2 in January, although record lows of -15 have been recorded. Snow can also occur during this period. March and April often switches between mild and cold weather. March sees temperatures between 11 and 5 degrees Celsius while April usually sees highs around 16 degrees Celsius and lows around 7 degrees Celsius. November is the wettest month in Sunny Beach, with temperatures between 13 and 6 degrees Celsius being typical. In October, temperatures between 19 and 12 degrees Celsius are usual.

Visit Sunny Beach in July or August if you want to experience the height of summer and the hottest beach parties. For a quieter holiday, consider booking your stay from the second part of May to June or during the month of September, when the weather is slightly cooler, but pleasant enough for a good vacation.

# Sightseeing Highlights

## Sunny Beach

Sunny Beach has over a hundred hotels and offers visitors a large selection of entertaining options. You can enjoy Go Karting, mini golf, horseriding and paintball. The Kuban hotel complex, at the very heart of Sunny Beach, has a casino, spa and tattoo studio. At its waterpark, you can cool off, as you navigate slides like the Kamikaze, the Braid and the Curving Dragon.

If you are in the mood for a spot of pampering, you can opt for Erna Spa. Therapies include Turkish bath, essential oils, massage, pedicure, manicure and beauty treatments.

The slingshot is located right on Sunny Beach Boulevard. Get strapped in with a friend and feel the adrenaline rush as you are propelled into the air at high speeds. Afterwards, you will be able to purchase a slow motion video capture of the experience. This attraction is open round the clock, seven days a week. For a slightly different kind of speed thrill, visit the Sunny Beach Karting track at the northern side of the resort, where you can race your friends in go-karts. The cost is 30 levs for ten minutes. The 18 hole mini golf course is beautifully laid out and practically on the beach.

## Action Aquapark

8240 Sunny Beach Resort, Sunny Beach Resort, Bulgaria
Tel: +359 554 26 235
http://www.aquapark.bg/

Although the Sunny Beach area has several waterparks, Action Aquapark boasts the longest and highest slide. This is the Uphill Navigator, a watercoaster which reaches a height of 20m. The slide is 165m long, but you will need to climb the 99 steps to get to the starting point. If you like speed try the Hydroshute with speeds of up to 60km and descent at a 70 degree angle, or the near-vertical drop of the Freefall slide. Brave the Black Hole for tunnels, curves, drops and special light effects. Relax in the wave pool, drift along the mellow Lazy River or sun yourself on one of numerous free sunbeds available. In the kid zone, young visitors can enjoy the fun of splashing water buckets on Adventure Island or hold water pistol shootouts on the multi-colored water castle

There is a petting zoo with a pony, peacocks, emus, mini pigs, pygmy goats and sheep as well as a gift shop. The Food Hall offers affordable fast food and drinks. Lockers are available for 5 levs per day. Action Aquapark is part of the Aqua Nevis hotel complex and guests of that hotel enjoy free access. For casual visitors, admission is 38levs for a full day and 19 levs for a half day pass. A free bus service to and from the park is available.

# Luna Park

Flower Street Sunny Beach, 8240 Sunny Beach, Bulgaria
Tel: +359 89 788 7519
https://www.tripadvisor.co.za/Attraction_Review-g499086-d3379465-Reviews-Sunny_Beach_Luna_Park-Sunny_Beach_Burgas_Province.html

Luna Park is centrally located at the heart of Sunny Beach. Kids can jump their hearts out on the SpongeBob trampoline or whirl round and round astride a swan or carousel pony. There are also bumper cars, teacup rides, mini golf and a shooting range. Strap up in the Looping Rollercoaster for a ride of your life as you whizz through a full 360 degree loop. Enter Horrorwood if you dare. The monsters, ghouls and ghosts inside are sure to give you chills.

# Khan's Tent

A slightly different style of entertainment can be found at Khan's tent, perched on a hilltop overlooking Sunny Beach. After an excellent dinner that is a little pricier than most of Sunny Beach, you sit back and enjoy an extravaganza of Bulgarian entertainment that includes high-kicking showgirls, acrobats, jugglers and comedians. The show usually wraps up at around 11pm.

# Sunny Beach Night Life

At the southern end of Sunny Beach, the Cacao Beach Club sets the pace. The club is popular round the clock and extends all the way to the beachfront. Cacao Beach hosts both local and international acts. It is the place to party on the beach. In this vicinity, you should also find the Bedroom Beach Club, one of the classiest establishments on the beach.

Disco Revolution on Flower Street bombards revellers with its spectacular sound and light design and the mixing skills of top resident DJs. Disco Orange is famous for its raucous paint parties. From May to September, Club Iceberg hosts top international guest DJs. Look for the large American vintage car near the entrance of Amigos. Inside you can choose from a large selection of cocktails. Den Glade Viking is themed around Scandinavian Disco and offers a great selection of house and trance music. The Flying Dutchman is the beach bar where Dutch visitors connect with their countrymen. It is open 24 hours and exudes a friendly atmosphere.

Guava Beach Bar/Guabba Beach Club is open throughout the day, but comes alive at night with exclusive foam parties, BBQs and dancing. Feeling thirsty? At Room 2 you can enjoy a limitless bar tab for a cover charge of 30levs, but do keep a little spare change for your bathroom breaks, which are charged. Why stay on land, though? The Tattoo Party Boat features a DJ station, dance floor, three bars and a lounge area to chill.

If you want to stay up to date on the trendiest events in Sunny Beach, download the Sunny Beach Life App (available from Google Play and other App Stores), which offers tips to parties, excursions, events and more. You can also tune into Sunny Beach radio, an English service for the latest in party news. Join the major league partygoers, by signing up for a bar crawl with companies like Party Patrol and Party Crew.

# Nessebar

Nessebar has a multi-facetted history that includes occupation by the Thracians, the Dorians the Athenians, the Romans, the Byzantines, the Bulgarians, the Crusaders and the Ottoman Empire. The town, also known as the Pearl of the Black Sea, even knew a brief spell as a quiet fishing village before its potential as a resort was realized during the 20th century. It has been declared a World Heritage site and considerable effort has been dedicated to restoration projects. Nessebar is an island, connected to the mainland by a narrow isthmus and from its cobblestone streets you can enjoy beautiful sea views.

Right at the heart of the Old Quarter, you will find the Church of Saint Sophia, the most ancient of Nessebar's churches. Also known as the Old Bishopric, it dates back to the period between the late 5th and early 6th century. Although it is a ruin today, with most of its relicts looted by the Venetians during the 13th century, Saint Sophia was once the seat of Nessebar's bishop.

The Basilica of the Holy Mother of God Eleusa likewise dates back to the 6th century and once belonged to a monastery complex. This church was damaged in an earthquake and its central nave and northern section became submerged. Thanks to restoration efforts during the 1920s, it has been preserved.

The Church of Saint John the Baptist dates back to the 10th century. It is a well-preserved cruciform church with a geospheric dome supported by four huge pillars. The Church of Saint Stephen is also known as the New Bishopric and its oldest sections date back to the 11th century. It has 200 murals, which depict scenes from the miracles of Christ as well as the life of the Holy Mother.

The Church of Paraskeva is noteworthy for its ornamental stonework which includes fish bone motifs and suns, as well as geometric zig-zags and checkerboard designs. It currently serves as an art museum. The Church of Christ Pantocrator can be found near the entrance to the Old Quarter. Dating back to the 13th or 14th century, it too is marked by beautiful ornamental stonework.

Most intriguing of these is the inclusion of swastika motifs, a medieval symbol for the sun. It too serves as an art gallery. Another church with splendid exterior brickwork is the Church of the Holy Archangels Michael and Gabriel.

Besides the Churches, there is an Ethnographic museum that offers insights into local crafts and trades, such as fishing and winemaking, as well as spinning and weaving. A room is dedicated to the character of the region's Thracian and Macedonian settlers. Another room features impressions by travellers to the region.

The Archaeological Museum exhibits a large variety of finds associated with the town's 3000 year history. These include coins from the 3rd century BC and stone anchors from the 12th century BC as well as pottery, lamps, urns, amphorae, statuettes and gold jewellery.

Active visitors will want to consider hiking from Sunny Beach. It is only 5.5km away. For less active tourists, there is a regular bus service connecting Nessebar to Sunny Beach, Ravda and Burgas. Boat excursions can be booked from the marina.

# Aqua Paradise

Tel: +359 55 460 016
http://www.aquaparadise-bg.com/

Aqua Paradise is located to the southwest of the Old Town of Nessebar and features a variety of thrilling water entertainment. For a ride that goes on and on, try the 146m Rafting slide. If you are looking for a high adrenalin rush, experience the Tsunami or the Kamikaze. Party at the Butterfly Pool, which offers a pool bar, pirate ship and dance floor, livened up with water streams. There is live entertainment every day from noon until 5pm, featuring dancers, a pirate show and games with audience participation. To relax, go to Paradise Island for two Jacuzzis and a range of hydrotherapies including underwater massage. There are free sunbeds and umbrellas. The kid's area has a water castle, complete with towers, slides, bridges and mazes to explore.

Photos and videos can be purchased from the Photo center and the Aqua Paradise also has a souvenir shop that sells T-shirts, beachwear, towels and sunscreen. Lifeguards are on duty and there is a first aid room. A free bus service provides connections to Nessebar, Sunny Beach, Saint Vlas and Elenite. A full day pass costs 40 levs and you can rent a locker for 3 levs or a safe deposit box for 5 levs. Once inside, the park uses a cashless system that lets you load spending money on a waterproof digital wristband.

# Sveti Vlas

Sveti Vlas is located about 5km north of Sunny Beach and its position, perched at the foot of Stara Planina mountain range, offers natural shelter from the prevailing north-eastern winds.

The town center is pedestrianized, with quaint little stalls selling jewellery and art. You can also expect occasional live entertainment. The main attraction is the Dinevi resort complex at the southern part of town, which includes an award-winning marina with berthing for up to 300 yachts.

The resort offers a variety of activities including volleyball, tennis, mini golf, yoga and fishing. There is a trampoline for kids, as well as casino, disco and live bands for adults. Yacht rentals, sailing lessons, canoe rental and wind surfing can be arranged. Beach umbrellas and sunbeds are hired out per day.

For a wide range of wellness therapies, visit the Asia Spa, which offers Turkish Baths, as well as Thai massage, Balinese massage, Philippine massage and Siberian massage. There is a fitness center, a Jacuzzi, hair salon, beauty salon, an ice fountain and a vitamin bar. Enjoy great views and a variety of drinks at the Cool & Hott Beach Bar or party in style at the Planet Yacht Club. Dinevi Marina hosts an annual regatta as well as a yacht exhibition.

## July Morning

If you are on the Black Sea coast in summer, you may want to consider travelling 150km north to Kamen Bryag in Kaverna to experience the sunrise on July 1st. It is a longstanding tradition in Bulgaria that is celebrated with a music festival.

During the repressive communist rule of Bulgaria, the song 'July Morning' by Uriah Heep became a rallying call for protest. Today, the song's composer John Lawton owns an apartment in Kavarna and regularly opens the July Morning Festival, an event to celebrate an era of freedom with its signature theme song.

A July Morning party also rocks the scene on Cacao Beach, by Sunny Beach.

# Lake Pomorie

Pomorie, Bulgaria

About 18km south of Sunny Beach, on the way to Burgas lies Lake Pomorie, famous for its black mud, which is said to have healing properties. The mud is considered beneficial for skin diseases as well as muscular and skeletal disorders. It can also be used as a beauty therapy.

Black mud can be found on the bed of Lake Pomorie, but many of the hotels and spas in the area offer the use of a balneological center, with a tub filled with black mud. Alternatively, you could run into a friendly local, who might offer to fetch you a bucket of mud for between 5 and 10 levs.

Lake Pomorie has a bird watching center and other attractions of Pomorie include a museum of salt, the Monastery of St George and the Thracian necropolis.

# Chateau Medovo

Medovo, Bulgaria
Tel: +359 887 818181
http://www.medovo.com/

If wine is your passion, consider a visit to a real Bulgarian winery. Chateau Medovo is located approximately 11km from Sunny Beach. It offers accommodation and is primarily a winery.

Choose from tasting packages focussing on classic wines, premium wines and spirits. These are priced between 20 and 40 lev and include snacks. Wine is also available for purchase.

# Burgas

Located about 38km south of Sunny Beach, Burgas is the second largest city on the Black Sea coast. It has its busiest port and is surrounded by three lakes, Vaya, or Burgas Lake, the largest, Atanasovsko Lake and Mandrenska Lake. All three are important bird watching sites, particularly during the migration period, and Mandrenska Lake provides access to the Poda bird watching zone.

A favorite recreation area for locals is the Sea Garden, a massive park laid out by the chief city gardener Georgi Duhtev around 1910. The park is filled with sculptures and monuments and offers beautiful sea views. The Mosta or bridge pier can be climbed to reach a viewing platform. There are various cycling and walking routes through and around the park, as well as a children's play area. There are usually performers and musicians in the park and, in the summer months, an annual Sand Fest attracts sand sculptors from around the world to delight visitors with their creations.

The Archaeological Museum of Burgas reflects a rich heritage of finds from in and around the Bay of Burgas. This includes Neolithic tools crafted from stone, flint and bone, Minoan style bronze ingots and coins and pottery from the ancient city of Deltum.

Of particular interest is the statue of Apollo, uncovered at the Antiy site as well as the treasures and religious objects recovered from the tomb of the Thracian priestess Leseskapra. To learn more about the folk art, crafts and dancing styles of the Black Sea region, visit the Ethnographic Museum. It hosts regular exhibitions and also presents a craft-related summer school. Burgas hosts two important music festivals in August. The Spirit of Burgas is a popular music festival that takes place towards Mid August, while the International Folklore Festival is held at the end of August.

# Sozopol

Sozopol is located on a rocky outcrop 35km south of Burgas. It was first settled in the Bronze Age and became a Greek around the 7th century BC. Sozopol thrived from trade and naval activity in the ancient world. By the 5th century AD, it was already Christianized.

You can learn more about the town's rich historical heritage at its Archaeological museum. Its large collection of exhibits include Greek vases, anchors of stone as well as lead, terracotta statuettes excavated from the Apollonia necropolis and a selection of medieval amphorae. One particularly intriguing exhibit is a reliquary believed to contain the bones of John the Baptist. This was uncovered on the nearby St Ivan's Island and probably came into the area via Constantinople.

Carbon dating and DNA analysis have revealed that the bones most likely came from a Middle Eastern male who lived in the 1st century AD. The museum is also home to another famous find of recent years. In 2012, the so-called Vampire of Sozopol skeleton was uncovered. This reputedly 700 year old male was buried with an iron stake through his left chest.

In the Old Town of Sozopol, as you stroll along its charming cobble stone streets, you will have the opportunity to view various examples of the historical Black Sea architectural style. Among these are Marieta Stefanova House, which was constructed right onto the medieval walls, Dimitri Laskaridis House, Kurdilis House (now also the location of the Ethnographic Museum), Kurtidi House (the Thracian Inn), Kreanoolu House, the House of Lina Psarianova and the House of Baba Kukulisa Hadzhinikolova. The walls date back to the 6th century, but have been rebuilt numerous times. Other historical structures include a small wooden well from the 4th to 3rd century BC, a Byzantine grain warehouse and a medieval chapel.

There are two main beaches, Central and Harmani Beach, as well as a camping area. Near the highway from Burgas, you should encounter Ravadinovo Castle, a fairy-tale castle that was constructed over the last 20 years. The grounds feature beautifully landscaped gardens as well as a lake with black and white swans. Sozopol hosts a film festival, the Appolonia Festival in the first week of September.

## Strandzha Nature Park

For a refreshing break from the beach party culture of Sunny Beach, consider a day trip to the Strandzha Nature Park. As one of the country's largest nature reserve, it is home to a diverse collection of indigenous animal species. These include over 50 mammal species such as wild boar, grey wolves, red deer, roe deer, golden jackals, red foxes, badgers, bats and wildcats and reptiles such as the European blind snake, the red whip snake, various turtles and tortoises and the sheltopusik or European legless lizard, the largest lizard species found indigenously in Europe.

The bulk of the park comprises of forest land and features Bulgarian plant species such as the Strandzhan oak, Caucasian whortleberry and Colchic holly that occur nowhere but in Strandzha. Some of its most ancient tree species such as the Oriental Sessile Oak trees, Oak trees and Oriental Beech tree include specimens that are over 500 years old.

A visit to the park will be particularly memorable to birdwatching enthusiasts as its coastal wetlands form part of the Via Pontica avian migratory route, the route followed by large numbers of Europe's storks and white pelicans, as they travel from Europe to Africa. Other bird species that may be views include the Eurasian Eagle owl, Egyptian vultures, olive tree warblers, Black kites, herons little egrets, sparrow hawks, osprey, grey and purple herons as well as the Black Sea's only breeding colony of spoonbill. To catch the migration in full swing, schedule your visit for the periods from mid May to early June or mid September to early October. The park usually presents specialized tours during the month of May.

There are cycling and walking routes of varying length throughout the park. While the scenic coastal routes will allow you to explore unspoilt beaches, hill walks may challenge your fitness level and reward you with stunning landscape views. Horse riding excursions can be organized from several villages including Brodilovo, Lozenets, Varvara and Sinemorets. Game fishing trips (including spear fishing or underwater fishing) can be booked in Sozopol. Various cultural fairs in the Strandzha region usually take place during summer and at the small village of Bulgari, you can observe the ancient ritual of Nestinarstvo or fire dancing. This usually takes place in the village square from sunset.

# Recommendations for the Budget Traveller

## Places to Stay

### Palace Hotel

Sunny Beach Promenade, Sunny Beach 8240, Bulgaria
Tel: +359 0554 22858
http://www.hotelpalace.bg/

The Palace Hotel is located right along the Sunny Beach Promenade, practically on the beach and only a few minutes walk from the popular Flower Street.

There is an a la carte restaurant with garden area, a children's playground and a mini convenience store, which is open 24 hours. The hotel also has a massage center, lobby bar, karaoke bar and a seasonal outdoor pool. Rooms include a flat screen TV and private bathroom with shower and complimentary toiletries. The hotel offers free Wi-Fi coverage, free parking and a laundry service. Accommodation begins at €25 and includes breakfast.

## Hotel Lotus

Sunny Beach, 8240 Sunny Beach, Bulgaria
Tel: +359 55 422 193
http://www.hotellotus.com/

Hotel Lotus is a small hotel, centrally located within a few minutes walk of the beach and also near the shops, restaurants, bars and clubs. There are several on site shops within the hotel, including a gift shop and a hairdressing salon. The hotel offers an a la carte restaurant, free parking and free Wi-Fi coverage. Rooms are spotlessly maintained and have satellite TV, a fridge, kettle and microwave. Accommodation begins at €25 and includes breakfast.

## Aparthotel Poseidon

Sunny Beach, 8240 Sunny Beach, Bulgaria
Tel: +359 55 424 411
https://www.tripadvisor.co.za/Hotel_Review-g499086-d1507175-Reviews-Poseidon_Apartments-Sunny_Beach_Burgas_Province.html

Aparthotel Poseidon is located at the quieter northern end of the Sunny Beach resort and is a 5 minute from the beach. The promenade is only a 2 minute walk from the hotel, although it takes about 30 minutes to reach the main strip. The hotel has an outdoor pool with poolside bar, a la carte restaurant and its own convenience store. Rooms include satellite TV, a private bathroom with free toiletries and a kitchenette with coffee machine, microwave and fridge. Accommodation begins at €30. Wi-Fi is charged separately at €9 per 24 hours.

## Ivana Palace Hotel

8240 Sunny Beach, Bulgaria
Tel: +359 55 424 130
http://ivanapalace.bg/

The Ivana Palace hotel is located at the western end of the Sunny Beach resort, about a 10 minute walk from the beach. It offers visitors an outdoor pool, with a separate section for children, as well as a play area, a fitness center that provides massage and sauna, a 24 hour medical center and conference facilities for up to 100 persons. Free Wi-Fi coverage is available in the public areas and the pool bar has a great selection of cocktails. Accommodation begins at €17 and includes breakfast.

## Hotel Avenue

Sunny Beach Resort, Sunny Beach, Bulgaria
https://www.tripadvisor.co.za/Hotel_Review-g499086-d579013-Reviews-Avenue_Hotel-Sunny_Beach_Burgas_Province.html

If a central location is your main priority, Hotel Avenue provides basic, but affordable accommodation. This small hotel is located about 100m from the Sunny Beach resort center and a 5 minute walk from the main strip and the beach. There is a fitness center, free parking and free Wi-Fi in all areas. Rooms are spacious and include a well-equipped kitchenette with microwave oven, fridge and coffee machine. There is also satellite TV and a private bathroom. Accommodation begins at €26.

# Places to Eat

## Morris Restaurant & Bar

On the beach, opp. Hotel Neptune, Sunny Beach, Bulgaria

With an idyllic location right on the beach and live entertainment at night, Morris Restaurant & Bar provides the right sort of ambiance to put you in a holiday mood. Despite its popularity, the service remains still efficient and friendly.

The food is tasty and good value for money. Meals include a good selection of seafood options such as sea bream, breaded mussels, grilled king prawn and salmon cutlets as well as pizza, burgers, pasta, salads, meaty grills, skewers and a selection of traditional Bulgarian dishes. Kavarna comes in a choice of chicken, pork or lamb and is served in a charming pottery dish. If you have a big appetite, try the mixed grill, priced at only 16 levs. Moussaka is 8 levs, the pork chop 12 lev and the roast chicken, 12 lev. Sports fans can enjoy live broadcasts on the big screen and the free Wi-Fi is an added bonus.

# Lapa Lapa Restaurant

Sunny Beach, Bulgaria
https://www.facebook.com/pages/Lapa-Lapa/203874753069267

Lapa Lapa is a family run restaurant that offers friendly service and generous portions. The wide selection of meal options include international favorites such as pizza, burgers, meaty grills, pastas and salad, as well as seafood dishes such as mussels, sea bass and shark steak. If you are hungry, sink your teeth into the mixed grill, which includes lamb skewers, chicken skewers, chicken fillet, ribs and chips. Another favorite is the roast lamb with mint sauce. The cocktails are affordable and quite strong. Expect to pay under 50 levs for a meal for two including drinks.

# Hawaii Restaurant & Bar

Main Promenade, in front of Hotel Glarus on the Northern side
Tel: +359 89 435 3411
http://www.hawaiirestaurantsunnybeach.com/

If you feel homesick for good old English grub, pay a visit to Hawaii Restaurant & Bar, located on the beach at the heart of the Sunny Beach resort.

One of the advantages is its budget friendly menu, which provides a good selection of meal options at under 15 levs. These include a full English breakfast (8 levs), Irish stew (10 levs), toasted sandwiches (10 levs), spaghetti Bolognese (13 levs), chicken skewer and chips (13 levs), pizza and chips (11 levs) and chicken or pork stir-fry (13 levs). You will also be able to enjoy pub favorites such as a shepherd's pie and chips or an ale pie. Portions are fairly large and English is spoken. There is also karaoke every night.

## Bolero Restaurant

Sunny Beach, 8240 Bulgaria
Tel: +359 55 431 081
http://www.bolero-restaurant.com/

Bolero restaurant is located 5 minutes from the beach and offers live music combined with diverse menu that includes pizza, sushi, seafood, grills and desserts. This family run restaurant has an attractive outdoor setting with comfortable seats. Available dishes include king prawns, lamb on a hot plate with mint sauce and the pear and goat's cheese starter. The lunch menu represents good value for money with most items priced at between 5 and 7levs.

## Djanny

Bazaar Palma, Sunny Beach, Bulgaria
Tel: +359 896-888-577
http://www.djanny.com/

Djanny is a popular eatery that offers diners a large and varied menu combined with friendly, efficient service and generous portions. Items on the menu include stuffed mushrooms, meat and chicken skewers, pizza, sea bass, halloumi and spinach cakes, pork ribs, goat's cheese with honey and walnut and shropska salad. Expect to pay between 15 and 25 levs per person.

# Places to Shop

## Royal Beach Mall

The Royal Beach Mall is one of the best shopping malls in Sunny Beach. It is located only 50m from the beach and forms part of the Barceló Royal Beach hotel complex. Leading fashion stores with outlets here include the Italian brand Ira-Maxima, Moncler, trendy Fetish, leisure wear from Doll & Cat, kid's fashion gear from Infano, underwear from Za-Za as well as shoes and hand bags from Sarah Pen, Aquamarine and La Scarpa.

Browse at Art House for unique, handcrafted jewellery items. At the Royal Beach Spa, you can enjoy massages and various other beauty therapies. Kedem offers a range of natural beauty products sourced from ancient medicinal plants and herbs found near the Dead Sea and includes a variety of rejuvenating creams, ointments, oils, sprays and tonics. While shopping, let your children join in a range of games and fun activities at Kid's Paradise.

# Sunny Beach Promenade

The Promenade of Sunny Beach is lined with numerous little stalls selling an assortment of branded clothing and accessories, ranging from sunglasses and trainers to football T-shirts and a variety of other gear. Do bear in mind that nearly all of these items are fake, but some are fairly high quality in manufacture and good enough to serve as holiday wear.

# Original Bulgarian Wine Shop

Tervel St. 6, Nessebar 8230, Bulgaria

Wine has been cultivated in Bulgaria for almost 3000 years, with local varieties of grape such as Rkatsiteli, Dimiat, Mavrud and Gamza being cultivated alongside better known varietals such as Chardonnay, Riesling, Sauvignon Blanc, Cabernet Sauvignon and Merlot. The climate and soils are very suitable for vineyards and with post-Communist privatization, the main focus shifted from mass production to the quality potential.

At the Original Bulgarian Wine Shop in the Old Town of Nessebar, you will be able to taste a good selection of local wines before making your selection. The shop also stocks the highly prized ice wine in white and red varieties.

## Ji'votnoto & Gallery

Mesambriya Street 34,
Near the Etnographical Museum,
Nessebar 8230, Bulgaria
Tel: +359 88 846 6604
https://www.facebook.com/jivotnoto.galleryTA

The wares on sale at Ji'votnoto & Gallery exude masses of rustic charm and quirky creativity. A wide variety of cheerful motifs and raw materials such as acorns and shells are used to craft souvenir items such as the colorfully decorated bells, handcrafted hair accessories, ceramics, hanging mobiles and other art.

Jewellery items include earrings, leather bracelets and colorful necklaces, while you can also purchase gift items such as bowls made of walnut wood or a half-winged angel for good fortune. The goods are sourced from local Bulgarian artists and craftsmen.

## Galleria Burgas

Yanko Komitov Str. 6, Burgas 8000, Bulgaria
Tel: +359 56 706 020
http://www.galleriaburgas.bg/

Galleria Burgas is the city's newest mall and you will find many famous international brands represented here. That includes Zara, United Colors of Benneton, H&M, Sportvision, Adidas, Nike, Esprit and Paolo Botticelli shoes. For the latest in electronics and tech supplies, visit Mediabox, iCenter or Technomarket. There is an outlet of Imaginarium, but you will also find a branch of Hippoland, Bulgaria's own chain of hypermarkets selling children's products.

For a spot of sensual indulgence, try Golden Rose, a Turkish brand of cosmetics or Perfumery Bargello, which stocks Turkish fragrances. Go to Timeland for luxury watches and jewellery and indulge your sweet tooth at Sugarland. For a wide variety of CDs, DVDs, toys, board games, puzzles and books, go to Ciela Books & Music. While the food court offers well-known names like Subway, McDonald and Burger King, you could also try OLA Taste of the MED for a selection of Mediterranean dishes. For fun, there is a bowling alley, as well as Fusion Motion and Playground for truly immersive gaming experiences.

Printed in Great Britain
by Amazon